Out of the Fog, Into the Sun

Out of the Fog, Into the Sun

My Journey from Hinduism to Christ

Jo Kinnard

RESOURCE *Publications* · Eugene, Oregon

OUT OF THE FOG, INTO THE SUN
My Journey from Hinduism to Christ

Resource Publications
An Imprint of Wipf and Stock Publishers
199 W. 8th Ave., Suite 3
Eugene, OR 97401
www.wipfandstock.com

ISBN 13: 978-1-60899-841-8

Manufactured in the U.S.A.

The scriptural quotations contained herein are from the New Revised
Standard Version Bible, © 1989, Division of Christian Education of
the National Council of the Churches of Christ in the USA. Used by
permission. All rights reserved.

To Mikey,
my husband and soul mate,
a prime example of God's grace

Contents

Acknowledgments

I AM deeply grateful to all my pastors, family members, and friends for encouraging me to share my faith story, articulating some of the questions with which I struggled as a seeker. In particular, I would like to thank: the Reverend Dr. John P. Nelson, the pastor who baptized me, for encouraging and enlisting me—right away—to use my gifts in writing and speaking as a witness for Christ; the Reverend Dr. Winston Persaud, my professor and advisor, for the teaching, guidance, and support that continually build me up and deepen my discipleship; the Reverend Dr. Duane Priebe, also my professor, for urging me to write about my experience because it was important to hear the testimony of people who were not "cradle Christians," and for taking the time to read my first draft; the Reverend James Winjum, my Clinical Pastoral Education Supervisor, for engaging me in many challenging discussions and expressing an interest in my writing; the congregations where I told my story in person, for inviting me and praying for me; my daughter Varsha, who now has her own amazing story to tell about her journey to Christ, for the many conversations we have had about God; and most of all, my husband Mike, for his steadfast love, companionship, and unswerving support—daily reminders of how deeply blessed I am. Praise be to God from whom all blessings flow!

Introduction

THIS IS the story of my personal faith journey. In this book, I share how I came to be a Christian, and why I am a follower of Jesus Christ. The story starts by describing a personal crisis that led me to realize that my spiritual center was empty. It goes on to tell how I reviewed my Hindu upbringing, and how my quest led me to become a Christian. It is a story I love to tell, and one that I have been blessed with opportunities to tell many times to both individuals and congregations. Each time I tell this story, I experience the same excitement and joy that I felt the first time I told it to my fellow congregants in the congregation where I was baptized: Hosanna! Lutheran Church, Saint Charles, Illinois. I am filled with the overwhelming reminder that God's grace has been so abundantly poured on me, even when I was completely unaware of it, through people, places, and circumstances.

This is a story that is meant to be shared, as a testimony to God's boundless mercy and love. Wherever you might be on the spectrum of seeking—atheist, agnostic, borderline or born-again believer, within or outside of Christianity—I invite you to be a part of my life, and witness for yourself the glory of God.

Christ's radical message has always provoked passionate discussion. There have been several books denouncing Christianity, and many more proclaiming it. The ranks of these writers have included philosophers, theologians, scientists, icons of pop culture, leading statesmen, and individuals such as myself. In 1927, the philosopher Bertrand Russell gave a talk[1] *Why I Am Not a Christian* that has since been published in different formats. More recently, theologian John Stott's book *Why I Am a Christian* appeared in print.[2]

In the next few pages, I share with you some of the many compelling reasons why I felt called to become a Christian. I discuss what it means for me to be a disciple of Christ, and how my Hindu upbringing and my exposure to other world religions provided a fertile ground of preparation for me, pointing me to Christ.

I did not come to Christianity because Hinduism was a shallow religion. Nor did I become Christian because I was marginalized in some way by my religion of birth. On the contrary, I was immersed in the best that Hinduism has to offer, earned a doctorate in one of the schools of Indian Philosophy that underlie Hinduism, and openly espoused this thinking. However, something was missing. Then, step by step, I was brought into the light and peace of God in and through Jesus Christ. I came to see what God's work in Christ means for our lives.

Most of all, this book is for those who, like the former me, are struggling to understand this nebulous thing called faith.

Jo Nageswaran Kinnard
June 2010

1. Russell, *Why I Am Not a Christian*, 3–23.
2. Stott, *Why I Am a Christian*.

1

Crisis

IN MY early forties, I was enveloped by the fog of a major personal crisis. The first thing to go wrong was the divorce. When it was over, I thought it was the worst thing that had ever happened to me. Painful as it was, I was determined to survive and rebuild my life. After the marriage had ended, my daughter and I had moved to a bigger city. I attempted to make a fresh start. Just when I thought I had it together again, my daughter—a "straight-A" kid all her life and the keeper of many of my dreams—dropped out of college in the fall of her sophomore year. This rejection of education, the very heart of my core values, would—in itself—have been sufficient to throw me for a loop. But to make matters worse, she joined a group of people that I could only regard as a cult. The leader of the group believed he was the second coming of Jesus. This did not bode well.

I had not seen this coming. From what she had told me, I had known that in her freshman year, my daughter was spending a lot of time hanging out with a group of anti-war protesters in Athens, Georgia, where she went to school. When she had first mentioned to me in the spring that she planned to spend her summer with some members of this group—cleaning up the streets of Athens—I had asked where she would be living. At this time, she was still in the dorm, but we had thought she would be coming home to her father or to me for the summer. She had mentioned that there was an old, empty house available, where it was expected that everyone involved in the "clean-up" would be staying. I was worried for her safety and did not really care for her new crowd, many of whom were homeless people. I was not worried about drugs or alcohol for she had always been very sure of herself, and verbal about those dangers. I was worried that she might be raped, abused, or murdered. I was worried that she might get sick. Worse, I feared that she might disappear. In addition, I had never actually met a homeless person, and my mind was filled with many prejudices about them. At the time, I saw the homeless as slackers who had chosen to live on the street, taking advantage of the compassion of hard-working people. I thought they were lazy, dirty, and unmotivated. I had no sympathy for them. So the idea of my daughter joining this crowd was morally and personally repugnant to me. I asked her where they would get the money they needed for their clean-up, and how she could be safe living on the street. She brushed my questions aside, expressing her belief that the universe would provide for these needs. Donations would appear when they were needed. She vehemently rejected the mind-set of the corporate machine to which, as she saw it, millions of other Americans and I belonged. She seemed to feel that all institutions were flawed, and desperately in need of an overhaul. She and her friends were seeking to return the world to a more loving and peaceful state—free from greed, and filled with hope.

If I set aside the over-simplification and generalizations in her words, I could not deny that there was some truth to what she was saying. It was not hard to see that many things were wrong with the world. However, all this sounded to me like typical teenage idealism and the rejection of the status quo. My heart was heavy, but I hoped that this was a phase that would soon pass. Knowing my daughter, there was little I could do about it anyway, and I trusted that she would develop some friendships in college that would be more appropriate for her. I still hoped to head off her summer plans when the time came. The summer arrived and my daughter spent time with each of her parents, but she also moved ahead with her stated plans, and spent some time with her new friends. She seemed none the worse for her experiences, and when the school year started, she returned to her dorm room. I was relieved that the school year was starting. She sounded very excited about her new classes. I heaved a huge sigh of relief.

When my phone rang a few days into the semester, I was not prepared for what I heard. I still remember the sinking feeling in my stomach when she informed me that she had dropped all her classes, and was moving out of her dorm room to live on the street with her new friends. I was assailed by a storm of emotions: shock, shame, dismay, fear, and anger. First, there were the concerns for her: Live on the street with a bunch of people much older than she was? That was crazy. This could not be happening! Sleep in a truck? Eat at the church? Shower at the mission? She was not homeless! She should not be doing this. Taking the vow of poverty and celibacy? (Thank God for the celibacy part!) Throw away her scholarship? Throw away her future? Then there were my own fears: I thought I had done everything right by this child! I had worked really hard to save my marriage, and when that had not panned out, her father and I had tried to avoid a messy, contentious divorce. Where did I go wrong? How could she do this to me? No! No! This was also a personal insult, and a rejection of everything for which I stood. How would I face up to other parents whose children were still in school? I was very angry with the man who led this group. I was sure he had brainwashed my daughter. The anger would persist for years. Jesus indeed! How could she be so blind? My anger was intensified by the fact that being Hindu at the time, I found the very idea of the second coming ridiculous. Now, this was a crisis.

Like most crises, mine had started long before I realized that my world was spinning out of control. A Hindu, I thought I was a believer. I even wore a necklace with an amulet of my favorite Hindu deity—Ganesh, the Remover of Obstacles. But somewhere along the way, I had lost touch with the meaning of faith, and the belief that there is a God who is actually listening when we call out for help. On the surface, I was still the person with the successful career. Inside, there was a yearning for something that seemed elusive and out of reach: peace. Although this was not apparent to me then, the crisis had not come out of the blue. It had been building for a while.

The pain of the divorce paled in comparison to the pain of watching my daughter throwing away her promising schooling—and potential career—and choosing the life of a homeless person. It was not safe for her on the street even if she thought she knew everyone, I pleaded. She was not homeless, I reminded her, and she was blessed with many gifts that she ought to use. She needed to be a provider, not a taker. I tried everything I could think of, including cold logic and heavy persuasion, but she would not be budged. I requested relatives to talk to my daughter. I requested a friend who was an elder in his Christian church to start a dialogue with her. These measures went nowhere. Weeks passed, and then months. The harder I tried, the further she moved from me. I was depleted, and angry. In desperation, I tried the "tough love" approach. This proved to be the last straw. My daughter dropped out of my world, and was almost entirely absent from it for several years. When we did see each other, it was virtually impossible to communicate. At times, I was sure I had lost her forever. To be torn from your child, I felt, was the mother of all crises. My heart cried, remembering that we used to be so close!

This was the start of the most desolate and painful period of my life. It is hard enough to deal with your teenage child leaving the nest, and becoming her own person. But when your child disappears from your life, wants nothing to do with you, rejects your core values, will not or cannot trust you, and wants to do things that appear to you to be dangerous and detrimental to her well-being, it feels as if your whole world is collapsing around you. You are overpowered by a tidal wave of negative emotions. The water never abates, and you feel like you are going to drown.

If this had happened in India, my parents would have been the first to hear of it, from me. This was the sort of crisis that would never be discussed openly outside the immediate family circle. For *Brahmins*, the caste to which I belonged, education is of paramount importance, and children were expected to be in school until they held a graduate degree in some field. In most Hindu families, the family would pray privately to one of their primary gods for a resolution. If a child was deemed to have gone astray, steps would probably be taken to forcibly bring the child home, and back to his or her senses. What had happened—the events surrounding the crisis—would remain a shameful secret never discussed at home or with anyone outside the home, with the exception of the family astrologer. For the family would contact an astrologer to find out whether, based on the child's natal chart, a particular alignment of planets was causing the problem in the first place. Planets were regarded as minor gods, and formed a significant subsystem of deities within the Hindu pantheon. Knowing that the child's behavior was a result of planetary conjunctions would make it possible to offer some gifts to the planetary gods to placate them, and bring life events back to normal. Even educated Hindu families continued to place their belief in such practices, viewing the universe as a system of interdependent forces.

I was not in favor of using force for a number of reasons. I recognized the harm that could do to my daughter's psyche. Even if I had tried to force her to change her plans, I could not have had any success, as she had reached the age of majority. Nor did I feel the need to go to an astrologer, though I am sure I could have found one on the Internet. I was torn between wanting her to be safe, and wanting to respect her boundaries. She was turning into an adult, and had the right to make her own choices, however poor they might seem. Yet in so many ways she was still a child, and as her mother, I could not help feeling that this was my fault. I felt trapped in a nightmare that would never end.

As for looking to my family as a support system, I was in America—oceans away from my mother. By this time, my father had died and my mother lived alone in India, and had many health issues, including high blood pressure. The last thing I wanted to do was to cause her to have a heart attack, from hearing that her favorite granddaughter had dropped out of college and worse yet, become a homeless person. I knew that my mother was planning a visit to the States, and would eventually find out what had happened, but I was not going to burden her with this over the telephone, across the oceans.

I turned to God, praying to the Remover of Obstacles for a resolution to this difficult situation. But somehow, this time, I could not feel the sense of confidence that my prayers were being heard. It was as if the faith I had taken for granted had disappeared. I had thought I was a believer, but I could not connect with God. All I could feel was a sense of utter despair and failure, and the knowledge that I had to handle this on my own. In my separation from my child, the crisis that changed my life forever was revealed. I came to the cold realization that I had no spiritual anchor to sustain me and that, without God to give me value, I was nothing.

But to help you understand how I had gotten to the point where I had lost touch with faith, I need to take you back to my childhood and my first steps as a believer.

2

Hindu Upbringing

I WAS born and raised Hindu in Madras (now known as Chennai), a densely populated city in southern India. The youngest of three children and the only girl, I was born about fourteen years after my brothers and was thus the baby of the family. My mother had prayed for a girl, and there I was. Because of the age difference between my siblings and me, I often felt I was an only child. In fact, my brothers left home early on in my childhood. I remained very close to my parents and was deeply influenced by both my mother and my father, in different ways. My mother was Maitili, and my father was Nageswaran, two of the most loving and accepting people I have ever known.

For most of my childhood, I grew up with plenty. My parents were well-to-do, and my needs and wants were more than adequately met. My mother was an extrovert who was an artist, a musician, and a great cook. She filled our home with beautiful paintings, needlework, music, and the sound of laughter. She celebrated life. She was a devout Hindu who cherished a personal relationship with God. The personal altar of Hindu deities to which she would tend daily was similar to those that can be found in every Hindu home. She would take great joy in celebrating all the Hindu festivals: making special eats for each deity, dressing them, decorating them with flowers, singing to them, lighting oil lamps and incense for them, and speaking to them. To her, all gods were worthy of adoration and praise. She was equally at home whether she was lighting a lamp to a Hindu deity on her altar, or lighting a candle in the Church of Infant Jesus, a Catholic shrine known for its healing power, and frequented by people of all faiths. In this regard, she was very different from the typical Hindu housewife.

My father was one of India's first small-scale indus-trialists, after the country got its independence from the British. After being educated in England, he had turned down a position with the British Broadcasting Corporation to return to India. He became an entrepreneur and started a business manufacturing radios, speakers, and other sound appliances. His hobby was mathematics, and in his spare time, he would ponder questions relating to such things as prime numbers. As the male head of the household, he did his part in religious festivities, but the intellectual and the skeptic in him frequently asserted themselves. He was a great storyteller. He would tell funny stories about the gods and goddesses in Hindu mythology and even encourage in us a certain irreverence for religious matters. I grew up in a household where it was acceptable to joke about God, and question tradition.

I was not *required* ever to go to the temple, but I always enjoyed going whenever we went. My family did not observe Hindu austerities such as fasting before certain feasts. Nor were our eating habits and table manners bound by rules of ritual purity. As I mentioned earlier, we belonged to the *Brahmin* or priestly (and teacher) caste. By the expectations of our particular caste, we were vegetarian but my parents never chastised any of their children for trying meat dishes at friends' homes. In fact, I was blissfully unaware of most orthodox Hindu practices until much later in life. Anything we practiced by way of religion was always in the realm of joy and personal choice rather than a requirement. My mother made feast days truly memorable with her emphasis on rejoicing rather than austerities. My parents took me on many road trips as part of pilgrimages to ancient, holy, Hindu temples. I had a culturally rich upbringing and easily identified with Hinduism in the way that it was presented to me by my parents.

My parents did not blindly accept Hindu traditional values. Because of this, I was saved from being party to discriminatory attitudes such as those based on the caste system, although I did not know this at the time. The caste system forms a definitive social hierarchy and is a central part of Hinduism. In ancient times, caste was based on occupation, and divided society into four primary groups: *Kshatriya* (warrior caste), *Brahmin* (priestly or teacher caste), *Vaisya* (merchant caste) and *Shudra* (laborer or servant caste), with a fifth category comprising those who did not fall within any of these castes, and were deemed "untouchables" or outcastes. Tribes that fell within this description have traditionally been ill-treated and shunned— forced to live in hovels on the outskirts of a town, made to step aside to let members of a "higher caste" pass, and denied equal education and employment opportunities.

Each of the major castes has multiple sub-castes and each has its own rituals and practices. Today the caste system no longer corresponds to one's occupation, but the rituals and cultural practices are still in place for the most part. Even within the Hindu scriptures, the concept of caste has been explained in different ways. In one interpretation, caste is determined not by birth but by one's aptitudes and dispositions.[1] For example, a *Brahmin* is anyone who is has a desire for knowledge, and is thus suited for teaching. A *Kshatriya* is anyone who has the aptitude for the martial arts and sports. Despite alternative ways to explain caste, the system has resulted in discrimination towards certain communities and in extreme cases even ostracism and marginalization. Since India gained independence, the government has tried to eradicate the caste system. Nevertheless, the caste system still holds its sway on Hinduism.

Growing up, I was aware that we were *Brahmins*, but the ugly side of the caste system remained largely hidden from me. I was free to have friends from other castes, stay over at their homes, and play and eat with them. Our household help, who were typically from the *Shudra* class, did not have to enter by a separate service entrance. In my parents' circle of acquaintances there were both *Brahmins* and non-*Brahmins*, and people of other faiths. In fact, I was free to befriend people regardless of caste, wealth, or social status. Both my parents and I enjoyed conversations with fruit vendors, chauffeurs, laborers, and random strangers we would meet in railway stations, and other places. I was allowed to hang out with the people my parents hired to work in the garden, cook, clean, and do odd jobs. These liberties made the world I inhabited a very different place from that of my

1. Swami Tapasyananda, *Srimad Bhagavad Gita*, 122. The *Bhagavad Gita* is a core Hindu scripture. The reference here is in chapter 4, verse 13.

peers, whose lives were far more regimented, with far fewer outside influences.

Ramasami, or "Mee" as I called him, was a blue-collar worker in my father's factory who worked in our garden on weekends. Mee told the best stories and was like an uncle to me. When his chores were done, we would eat lunch together seated side by side. This was a radical thing to do in those days and possibly even today. There are strict rules for social conduct that would prevent such intercaste, interclass interaction. Although *Brahmins* emphasize intellectual accomplishments and prefer white-collar jobs, my parents recognized the dignity of manual labor.

From a practical standpoint, one's birth into a particular caste still defines who one is, whether one will get a seat in college, whom one will marry, and how one will live one's life. Even the more educated Hindus remain bound by these traditional mores, which tend to be a matter of pride. My parents were among those who were the exception to this rule. Most *Brahmins* in those days used the caste name as their last name but my father did not follow this practice. Even so, our family's caste identity as *Brahmin* was not hard to tell, because we spoke Tamil with a *Brahmin* dialect. We took pride in our *Brahmin* heritage, without needing to subscribe to its undesirable aspects.

A fair complexion is widely regarded as a minimum requirement for someone to be considered beautiful, particularly among *Brahmins*. Prejudicial attitudes that are based on skin color are not exclusive to white people. They are signs of human brokenness, and are universal. Thanks to my mother, I was always made to feel beautiful, although my skin is as brown as it gets. Although my parents had an arranged marriage, common in India even today, they were made for each other. My father's sisters did not approve of the match because my mother was dark-skinned in comparison to my father's lighter coloration. My father dismissed his sisters' comments and married my mother anyway. My parents believed that all people are equally worthy of respect regardless of skin color, caste, or any other criteria, and taught me to vehemently shun the scourge of untouchability.

I first learned about God from my parents. My parents' home had a beautiful altar housing a variety of Hindu gods and goddesses, decorated anew with flowers each morning. Some of the gods and goddesses were anthropomorphic depictions, characters such as the king Rama from Hindu epics such as the Ramayana. Others were imaginary creatures—combinations of man and animal—such as Ganesh, who has a human body and the head of an elephant. Yet others were animals such as Hanuman, the monkey-god who is another character from the epic Ramayana. Hanuman represents the attitude that one can accomplish anything to which one sets one's mind. I was taught that I could pray to any of these gods, one in particular that appealed to me, or all of them. I learned at an early age from my parents that none of these deities made of wood or stone or captured in other artwork were actually God. They were representatives, artistic conceptions, or symbols for the one, ineffable God. God was too big and too hard for ordinary mortals to understand, and too complicated to fit into any human idea. This made sense to me at the time, and I was pretty sure that the same God was everywhere—on the altar at home, in the Hindu temple, and in the chapel at school. Even so, we worshipped at home and at temples in a predominantly polytheistic way, for it was easy to slide from "speaking as though God is many" to speaking to different gods and goddesses. It was also hard to reconcile arguments between Hindus who worshipped one god or goddess exclusively over others, and maintained that their god or goddess was the greatest.

My involvement with God as a child was primarily in the context of making requests through prayer. A typical Hindu way to pray is to ask for something in return for an offering. The most common offering was a coconut, which would be presented in the temple—in the name of the requestor or in God's name—as soon as the request was granted, or sometimes beforehand. Sometimes much bigger offerings would be made, depending on the requestor's abilities or the nature of the request. There seemed nothing wrong about this barter. After all, if God is seen as Father or Mother, it is perfectly natural to ask for this or that to be granted. For example, my mother would often talk to the deity Murugan, saying: "If my child's fever is lifted, I will make you your favorite sugar pudding." The fever would break, and the pudding would be brought forth. After it had sat for a few minutes in front of Murugan, we would share the rest of it since—by now—Murugan had had his fill.

The offering was seen as a form of giving thanks, rather than an exchange for services rendered. In Hindu mythology, God takes on many *avatars* or incarnations, human and otherwise. However in these *avatars*, God remains God, and wholly other. Although God assumed a form, God did not enter into the form to the extent of suffering the downside of being a created being. Thus, I had a sense of God as being removed from the world although interacting with it through the incarnation. God was not someone with whom I could have a two-way conversation, as with a friend. It was clear that I needed to be faithful to God, but that God was not subject to such human descriptors as "faithful." To call God "friend" was considered presumptuous.

Sometimes, to play it safe like other Hindus did, I would pray to numerous deities in the hope that one or the other deity would grant what I was fervently requesting. The contradictions rising out of the Hindu concept of God, which for some was polytheistic, for others monotheistic, and for many both, were an integral part of my Hindu inheritance. These growth experiences led to much searching and pondering in my youth and early adulthood, as I tried to formulate my understanding of God in response to life situations.

An important but often unstated assumption underlying Hinduism—and many other eastern religions—is the belief that the present life is only one of many countless lives each individual will live, as the soul transmigrates through the cycle of birth and rebirth, in different embodied forms—plant, animal, or human. This is closely tied to the theory of *karma*, a term that is now widely and loosely used in conversation even outside Hindu circles in terms of "good *karma* " and "bad *karma*," thanks to the Internet and the globalization of world cultures. This is the belief that all actions, good or bad, have consequences for the doer of the action. *Karma*, as understood in Hinduism, runs much deeper. It has an impact on our predispositions and the choices we make, because the actions that we perform leave impressions on us that we carry through our numerous births. *Karma* also determines what happens to us, whether now or in a future life. The theory of *karma* provides a way to understand why bad things happen to good people, as when an innocent child is stricken with brain cancer, or why one person is born into wealth, while another is born in a slum. Thus, by living my present life in a virtuous manner, I increase the chances of being born in my next life into a better condition, one that is more conducive to facilitating my eventual escape from the cycle of rebirth altogether.

Furthermore, each individual is responsible for working out his or her own redemption. Most schools of Hinduism agree that *karma* is not fatalism, because one can change the future course of one's life and rebirth by one's present actions. The consequences of past actions, however, cannot be avoided. God's role in the matter of *karma* is not clear. From one perspective, *karma* offers a unique way to look at the problem of evil. From another, even God cannot save a person from living out the effects of his or her own actions. In my youth, I really liked the idea that, because of *karma*, I controlled my own destiny. I brushed away its implications for a concept of God.

Hinduism does not regard life in any embodied form—human or otherwise—as a desirable state because embodiment inevitably involves pain and suffering. Liberation from the cycle of birth and rebirth is the ultimate value for a Hindu, as it offers release from all pain and suffering. Such release, however, is only possible from a human life-state. Thus a person must work hard to gain liberation by reducing one's *karma*, both good and bad. There is a way to get out of this cycle of birth and rebirth. The different schools of Hinduism do not fully agree on the nature of this liberation, or how it might be obtained. For the theistic schools of Hinduism, where God's grace is the sole means of release, liberation is treated as synonymous with salvation, and means dwelling in blissful communion with a particular god in paradise. In at least one school of Hindu thought, there is a belief that some souls are eternally damned and will never experience this kind of liberation or salvation. Within the Vedanta, which represents the most systematized Hindu thinking, the monistic school of Advaita has been studied in depth by thinkers from the West. Here, liberation is obtained by knowledge when the soul realizes that its true nature is not embodied, and merges into the one, indivisible reality or Absolute, which, because all words fall short, is called "existence-consciousness-bliss" or Satchitananda.

My parents subscribed to the theory of *karma* and to the idea of transmigration and so did I, growing up as a Hindu. Of the many names I was given, one is my paternal grandmother's, for it was generally believed that her soul had been born again in my body. Or to put it differently, I was my grandmother in my previous life. Once again, thanks to my parents' liberal views, we frequently joked about such things. Despite the jokes, I think we really believed that we would pass from one life to another until we obtained liberation. My mother, however, was not interested in liberation. She said she loved life and was glad to be born again and again in different bodies. Some in my family believe she has come back after her death. They believe she has been reborn as my grandniece, and fully expect to see my mother's many talents in the latter.

The concept of transmigration on a practical level disposes Hindus to take a very cosmic view of time in general. It is as if to say that things will eventually work themselves out, in this lifetime or the next. This attitude about time makes itself felt in day-to-day dealings, at home, in school, and in the workplace. What might be accomplished in weeks takes months, or even years, because there is no sense of urgency whatsoever. My mother was definitely the exception to this rule. She had no time to waste. After she efficiently took care of all her chores, her cooking, and her commitments for the day, she had time to pursue her hobbies, which included sewing, music, painting, and tennis. She could not bear to waste a single day.

Karma is not the only thing that influences one's life, by attaching matter to the soul, which is in reality nothing but pure consciousness. Among the lesser deities worshipped in a temple are planetary gods such as Saturn, and the Sun. As briefly alluded to earlier, Hindus believe in astrology and the impact of planetary configurations on one's fortunes, based on the natal chart under which one was born. Finding a mate, arranging a wedding, buying a house, and other important events are best not carried out until after ensuring that the persons, the date, and the time are appropriately matched based on the natal charts of the concerned individuals and their governing planets. In times of job loss, illness, death, or other calamities, Hindus take guidance from astrologers on the gods that must be propitiated because they can influence the planet in question to reverse its ill effects.

Despite their more rational leanings, my parents believed in astrology. When times were difficult, they would consult an astrologer and take comfort in offering placatory gifts to the planet that was causing their woes. I accepted it unthinkingly as a child, but as I grew older, it was hard to explain away. It seemed to put a dent in what otherwise seemed to be a solid religion.

My awareness of these matters was heightened by the fact that in college I studied philosophy and religion. I found this field of study so fascinating, that I went deeper and deeper, eventually earning a doctorate in Indian Philosophy, specifically in Advaita Vedanta. My doctoral dissertation examined the concept of the person in Shankara (a ninth-century thinker who is regarded as the foremost exponent of Advaita) and compared it to that of Jean-Paul Sartre (the well-known twentieth-century French existentialist). I was fortunate in having the best scholars in my field as my teachers at the Dr. S. Radhakrishnan Institute for Advanced Study in Philosophy, at the University of Madras. Here I had the opportunity to question my beliefs, through a close and critical examination of the underlying principles of Hindu thought. I was exposed to the finest minds from centers of philosophical excellence all over the world, who came to my school to present their ideas, papers, and writings. Thus, as a Hindu, I was not just born and raised in that religion. I also fully accepted and lived the core tenets of Hinduism, because of my investment in its study, an investment I expected would lead to my deployment as a professor and scholar of Hindu Philosophy.

Before we go too far into the higher education that shaped me as a Hindu, there is another important area of my faith story that I must share, because it offers a striking contrast to my Hindu background. In the next chapter, I talk about my exposure to Christianity as a child, teenager, and young adult, and how—at the time—I dismissed it.

3

First Exposure to Christianity

THE MADRAS of my childhood was already a huge metropolis and, as one of the earliest British strongholds, well-endowed with a University, many fine schools and colleges, and exposure to Western culture. Madras boasted many libraries, including that of the Theosophical Society, the British Council, and the United States Information Service. Leading dance, drama, and musical troupes from all over the world made Madras a stopping point on their tours. Madras offered centers for learning foreign languages through such organizations as the Alliance Française and the Goethe Institute. It was thus a window to the world. Thanks to my parents, I grew up in a culturally diverse milieu with a strong emphasis on learning that extended to schooling, sports, and the fine arts. Madras was also a center of much Christian missionary work. It contained many old churches, including one in Mylapore, the orthodox Hindu neighborhood where Saint Thomas, the apostle who brought Christianity to that part of the world, is said to have been murdered. Mylapore is also one of the centers of *Brahmin* orthodoxy in Madras.

In those days, parents who were serious about education would enroll their children in Catholic institutions.

From kindergarten through high school, I attended the Convent of the Good Shepherd, a school for girls run by Irish nuns. The medium of instruction was English, which even today is one of the many official languages in India. Our principal, Mother John (later called Sister John), was a strict disciplinarian who ran the school with an iron fist. Following her cue, many of my teachers were sticklers for attention to detail, neatness, and obedience. Each morning one of the nuns would ring the school bell by hand, a sign that we needed to stop playing in the school yard and start gathering in front of the school building for assembly and prayer. The line-up started with us marching briskly, two by two, in step with Sousa's "Stars and Stripes Forever," being played over a loudspeaker in the yard. Even today, when I hear this march played, the memories of my school years come rushing back to me. The music transports me to a different time and place: I am standing in formation facing the school steps where Mother John is waiting to lead us in prayer.

Whether or not we were Christian, we all had to memorize and recite the Lord's Prayer every morning. After prayers and announcements, there was an inspection of attire and shoes. Our white uniforms had better be a dazzling white, not a dull white. Our white shoes had better be polished with the right shoe polish, not hastily covered over with white chalk dust. Our hair had better be in neat braids with red ribbons. We had better not be missing our red school ties with badges. Our nails had better be neatly clipped, and we had better not be wearing any make-up or nail polish. Those who failed to make muster would be punished, with the punishment ranging from memorization and recitation of long English poems to some other, more onerous writing assignment. Occasionally when the nuns were in a good mood, we might get off with a light rap on our hands with a ruler. The nuns firmly believed in the motto: Spare the Rod and Spoil the Child. Consequences for failing to do one's homework ran along the same lines. One might get imposition (the sentence "I will remember my p's and q's" written one hundred times neatly in straight lines), detention (remaining at school an hour after school was dismissed), shaming (standing on your bench throughout the class period), or probation (standing outside the school building in the sun all day long pending possible expulsion from school). Only God could save you from the wrath of Mother John if you were bold enough to be late.

Mother John's methods, harsh as they were, were effective as far as preparing us for academic excellence in college was concerned. I do believe that she was motivated by the desire to see "us natives" get a firm grounding in reading, writing, and arithmetic. I did not appreciate the discipline, but despite everything, the teachers and nuns instilled in me a deep love of learning, and a desire to try to excel in whatever I do, both of which still motivate me today. Mother John and her coterie of Irish nuns were deeply passionate about their Christian mission of bringing education to a country far different from their own home. They tried their best to teach about Christ at every opportunity. Most of the students were Hindu—and despite the missionary emphasis—remained Hindu. Hindu parents who sent their children to Catholic institutions were quite sure that the children would receive a great education. They were not in the least bit afraid that the efforts to convert their children to Christianity would succeed. If anyone had suggested then that I might convert to Christianity some day, I would have laughed hysterically. Nothing could have been further from my mind, or my parents' minds. It was impossible, and would never happen.

For one thing, no amount of missionary indoctrination at school could override Hindu traditional values practiced at home. More importantly, there was an underlying assumption that most of us Hindus held: there could not be any religion greater than Hinduism. We Hindus felt that we had the direct line to God. We did not need a middleman. And for us, Jesus was just that. So when the nuns insinuated that Hinduism was seriously flawed, polytheistic, and idolatrous, we simply did not pay any attention. Neither our parents nor we took the nuns' teachings about God seriously. We were convinced that Christianity was a religion in its infancy, compared to a mature and established religion such as Hinduism that had survived for an eternity.

I did not learn about the love and acceptance of Jesus Christ from Mother John, but it was at the school chapel that I first experienced the sense of awe and wonder about God, the creator, redeemer, and sustainer of the universe. The chapel was a wonderful place to connect with the mystery of God—unlike the majority of Hindu temples that I visited. Hindu temples were typically noisy, crowded, and disorderly. My response of awe to the tranquility of the chapel at school is another indicator of something common to all humanity, no matter what continent provides the soil for one's growth. The chapel was a beautiful, tranquil building on campus that always had its doors open for anyone who wanted to visit. It was a quiet, dark place, lit only by candles. The floors were made of clean, cool, polished mosaic tiles, and surrounding the pews were life-size statues of Jesus, and Mary, and the Stations of the Cross. The altar was beautiful with a life-size crucifix. The gentleness and compassion in Christ's eyes had a calming influence on me as I knelt there trying to pray like my Christian classmates, when we visited the chapel during lunch break. No one said a word, not even a whisper. We would just dip our hands in the holy water chalice at the entrance and then proceed to quietly kneel and pray. I remember praying that I would pass my examinations, or be saved from Mother John's disapproval. I might also have prayed that I would grow up quickly and escape from her clutches. I thought Jesus was a great man, and was not quite sure why he was crucified. But even then, I knew that somewhere in that chapel, God was listening to me. Once we were back outside in the sunlight, the magic of that moment vanished quickly and I was keenly aware of the demands being made on me by Mother John.

Through school and Christian friends, I learned many Christian hymns, and participated in nativity pageants and door-to-door caroling at Christmas time. There was a sizeable Anglo-Indian community in Madras, families that were the result of inter-marriage between Indians and British people during the colonial period. The Anglo-Indians we knew were primarily Catholic, had British names, dressed in western attire, and spoke British English with a distinctive accent. Over time there had evolved a new Anglo-Indian dialect—a form of English with numerous native words that had now become anglicized, and were a part of the language. Because of their preference for their British cultural heritage, Anglo-Indians were often set apart in independent India, and tended to keep to themselves.

In a country where caste is all-important, they were often ridiculed by so-called full-blooded Indians for their inadequate pedigree. Traditional Hindu women in Madras wore saris—six yards of material draped over a long skirt and short blouse—and regarded dresses that revealed arms and calves as too revealing and even indecent. Typically, Hindus did not freely mingle with Anglo-Indians on a social level but—once again—my parents did not fit the norm.

The Smith sisters were Anglo-Indians and close friends of my mother. We would frequently share meals at each other's homes, and during these visits, the sisters would lay hands on our heads and pray to Jesus for our welfare. We loved the Smith sisters and politely endured their prayers. Once out of earshot, we would express our true feelings by laughing aloud. We could not help ridiculing their efforts to pray over us. We simply could not understand why they felt compelled to do so, with the laying on of hands. After all, we did not pray over them! This kind of intercessory prayer was alien to Hindu tradition, where prayer is an individual matter. As mentioned before, it was also puzzling to us that a man named Jesus was being used as an intermediary to talk to God. At the same time, however, my parents openly and deeply appreciated the hospitality of Christian homes.

Most of the teachers at reputable schools in those days were from the Anglo-Indian community. The world these teachers, and my principal Mother John, created for me was in sharp contrast to the life I enjoyed at home. The overriding difference was religion. For the most part, the nuns treated those of us who were "heathens" with patience and forbearance and tried hard to convert us to Christianity. Mother John's rhetoric was loaded with placeholders for sin, guilt, punishment, and penance. She made Christianity sound like a prison camp. I had some classmates who were Christian and they frequently *had to* do certain things such as going to church on Sunday, attending catechism, and so on. I was smug about the fact that, as a Hindu, I was free from such obligations.

My attachment to Hinduism was further strengthened by my encounters with Christian missionaries. It was difficult to understand the Christian passion for evangelism. Madras was full of Christian missionaries. Some of them would go door to door distributing Bibles. Others would seek out prospective converts at schools, clubs, and other public places. It seemed as if they were everywhere. We wished they would leave us alone. The story of baby Jesus' birth was really lovely. It reminded us of the story of the birth of Krishna, a Hindu deity. Just like Herod who killed all the male children in Judea, Kamsa is a king in Hindu mythology who ordered killed every child that might have been an incarnation of God coming to kill him. The story of Jesus dying on the cross, however, was beyond our comprehension. The Christian missionaries told us we were and would always be sinners. This went against the Hindu belief that the soul in itself is pure, and can return to a state of perfection once we get rid of the results of our *karma*. They also talked about Jesus dying for our sins, about our having one life to live, and about our going to heaven when we died. None of this made any sense to us Hindus, since we believed in rebirth and transmigration of the soul. We expected to be born over and over again in different bodies. Heaven and hell were regarded as transitional states between these births.

As a teenager approached by a missionary eager to share the good news with me, my impulse was to run in the other direction. Like so many people who regard religion with skepticism, I concluded that Christianity was a form of brainwashing, and the church an institution created to control society. For who in their right mind would want to submit to a set of creeds and commitments, modeled after a person who had given up his life when he might easily have changed course? And why would the self-sacrifice of one individual matter to me anyway? It seemed to me that there could be no religion equal to Hinduism in its breadth and depth of perspectives, and its ability to reflect the individual seeker's spiritual leanings and predilections.

The missionaries I encountered were mostly of the hellfire-and-damnation variety and seemed intent on saving us from a fate worse than death. We did not want to be rude, and so we remained watchful and just ran in the other direction if we spotted a missionary headed our way, armed with Bibles or handouts. Even so, Bibles were handed out at school and in colleges and other public institutions many times during the year. Our home had more than one copy of the Bible, and I remember reading it at an early age. It was a fascinating story, with a lot of strange names. Because the missionaries were not inspiring, they often became the object of private jokes. They pushed me away rather than pulled me toward understanding Christianity.

In hindsight, I can see that the very character of Hinduism that I once so loved—its all-encompassing nature—is fractured at its core. It is not possible to be all things to everybody without losing one's identity. Still, I became more and more entrenched in Hinduism. By the time I was eighteen, I was quite smug in my belief that in its breadth and depth, Hinduism was unmatched by any other religion. If someone had engaged me in conversation on this topic, I would have vehemently denied that I had a bias. I was sure that my Hindu leanings were a result of careful, intellectual cogitation, rather than upbringing. By this time, I had started becoming aware of the problematic nature of some Hindu beliefs. I was aware that every religion has sticky issues, but I was convinced that only Hinduism—because of the depth and breadth of the varieties of philosophical thinking included within its systems—could provide consistent and complete answers to our deepest questions about God, about ourselves, and how we stand in relation to God.

It was not until I was a teenager that I began to realize how different my family's social mores had been than those of traditional Hindus. Even then, I did not fully appreciate my parents or my lenient upbringing. Nevertheless, the individualistic nature of Hinduism, the way my parents gave room for personal explorations in the spiritual realm, and the absence of religious requirements made me quite content to be Hindu. After I moved to the USA, I continued to visit Hindu temples where available, and practice Hinduism on my own at home.

The idea that there can be many conceptions of God is beguiling. It acknowledges that each individual meets God in a different way in a different place. However, we forget that the limits are ours, not God's, as the human mind tries to wrap itself around the infinite. Torn between perspectives that are hard to reconcile, it is easy to become lukewarm about our response to God. Forgetting that God is the ground of our very existence, we take refuge in rhetoric and arguments, and settle for a supreme being that lives solely in our minds. And when our mental construct cannot deliver what we think we need, we toss it altogether. We then fill the void with worldly things we think we can control.

In my encounters with Christian missionaries, neither side wanted to listen to the other. Instead of agreeing that there could only be one true God, we both reacted as outsiders to the other's religion. We did not first establish our presuppositions and then proceed to talk about God. There was never any dialogue in these encounters. The closer they pressed, the farther I drifted. The person telling me about the Christian God was probably familiar with the gods and goddesses of Hinduism as seen worshipped in Hindu temples everywhere, and not surprisingly, must have determined that Hinduism is strictly polytheistic, and idolatrous. My understanding was entirely different, based on what my parents had told me.

I could not understand why we—Christians and Hindus—could not just agree to keep our own separate supreme beings and each go our own way. It would be years before I had thought through the intellectual or practical ramifications of the concept of God. As I grew older, I began to revise my understanding of God, based on schooling, Hindu scriptures, the answers provided by fellow Hindus, social life, and through my interactions with fellow Hindus in worship. I found that the views of my Hindu relatives and friends were by no means identical to mine. The fact that Hinduism included multiple schools of thought on God, including polytheism, pantheism, and monotheism gave me pause, for the matter of God in Hinduism was no longer as simple as I had imagined. For the most part, I just suppressed or ignored these first stirrings of awareness about the contradictions within Hinduism. There was also the prevalent notion among the more educated Hindus that the polytheistic and mythological front presented by Hinduism was meant for the masses. Those who were gifted with intellectual prowess would be able to see through this to the true meaning of God in Hinduism, as expressed by the seers and mystics of the Upanishads. This elitist argument was appealing and I latched onto it, regarding myself as one of the intelligentsia. I conveniently ignored the social underpinnings of such an ideology. It seemed unimportant that the vast majority of Hindus were stuck in polytheism and idolatry, never moving on to a realization of the one God.

My explorations of major religions from an academic perspective were undoubtedly instrumental in my formation as a Hindu of Advaitic orientation. I found myself slowly drifting toward the belief that the idea of a personal God was ultimately a fiction, a crutch that we create. Far from being alarmed by this idea, I found it more and more compelling, particularly because Advaita Vedanta seemed to support and explain this understanding in a coherent and satisfactory manner. Christian theologians interested in understanding Hinduism have continued to study this influential school. Advaita offers the most analytical and internally consistent account of any of the systems of Hindu thought. Advaita holds that our unhappiness is a result of our mistaken identification, through ignorance, with the plurality of the world, when in fact we are non-different from a universal consciousness, also called *Brahman* (not to be confused with *Brahmin*, the name of the caste to which I belonged).

To an Advaitin, the idea of an individual self and a deity that one worships, as distinguished from this non-dual consciousness, is an illusion. The very idea of a personal god must, in the final analysis, be left behind in order to embrace one's true nature. In grasping one's nature as this non-dual consciousness, all intermediaries are discarded. The logic of this position led me to confront the fact that if I started with these pre-suppositions, all I had to rely on was myself, and that was adequate. I set myself to work on expanding the knowledge that would set me free. I was convinced of the validity of this school of Hinduism. I was living it, proclaiming it, and after earning my doctorate in this field, professionally defending it. I was even more staunchly Hindu than I had been in my childhood, because now, I was choosing Hinduism, after having examined it closely. On another level, unbeknownst to me, I was changing in ways that would not come to light until I had survived my crisis. I was turning into an intellectual to whom faith would soon be a stranger. Knowledge for the sake of knowledge was attractive. Knowledge was becoming my idol.

It might seem that despite spending eight hours a day, five days a week in a Christian school, I persisted in my Hindu convictions. It might appear as if none of what I heard about Jesus Christ made any difference to me. I do believe, however, that the message of Jesus was already being heard by me, and being stored in some deep recess in my mind. I would continue to make connections between what I was hearing, learning, and feeling, and some day it would all come together.

By the time of the crisis, I am already in a state of ambivalence about the idea of believing in God, although I had not acknowledged this in a conscious manner.

4

Fog

BEFORE MY separation from my child threw me into the vortex of self-pity, self-loathing, anger, disappointment, and guilt that I described earlier, I had thought I had things well under control. Life was good. In my BA, I had studied the major world religions, including Christianity. By now, I had four graduate degrees: two MAs (Eastern and Western Philosophy), my PhD in Indian Philosophy, and a MS in Computer Science that I had added after coming to the USA. When I had first arrived, it had not been easy to find a teaching job in Philosophy in the city where I lived with my family, but the Information Technology (IT) industry was bursting at the seams with jobs. Practical considerations and my love of logic had led me, with more schooling, to pursue a career in Information Technology. I was making good money. Through all my problems and past the divorce, I persisted in my belief that I was perfectly capable of doing my own philosophical explorations into the deeper questions of life. I read widely, picking from Western and Eastern thought, believing that I had an open mind.

Now that my foundations had begun to crack, I tried to reformulate what had become my own unique concept of God. For a Hindu this is not a radical idea. After all,

Hinduism is an amalgam of different strands of thinking, ideas that have continued to come together from diverse sources since time immemorial. By its very nature,
Hinduism allows for this kind of exploration within its vast
domain. My understanding of God or Ultimate Reality was
a combination of ideas and concepts that were convenient
for me to adopt and, although I did not recognize this, for
the same reason did not really have a firm basis. I pulled
together different devotional and intellectual threads from
Hinduism until I had a God of sorts. My God was not anthropomorphic, but a kind of nameless energy of which everything and every living being was a part. Such a concept is
not far from the ideas expressed in many Eastern religions.
My goal in salvation was to dissolve my individuality into
that energy, to exist in a state of bliss that was beyond both
pain and pleasure. This ideal of salvation was said to be at-
tainable based on the Upanishads. I was not yet able to see
that my framework had serious flaws.

I started by thinking about faith as I knew it in my
childhood. In my solitary spiritual ponderings, I often felt
a disconnect. I could not reconcile the sense of awe I felt
about the universe with my inability to rationally explain
the idea of faith. I tried to experience my mother's comfort
with the gods and goddesses of my childhood and her powerful, yet simple, devotion. It just did not seem to work for
me. It seemed to be a one-way relationship, and I was never
sure where I stood in relation to a given deity. I had grown
up in a world that was very different from that in which she
had been raised. She was an artistic soul, very comfortable
with Hindu mythology. She was not drawn to theology or

discussions about God, the world, or our relationship to God.

Next, I considered my father's more intellectual take on spirituality. To him, God was wholly other, and completely outside human conception. A God with whom one might have a personal relationship was a figment, a mental crutch at best, although a very useful one. I had taken refuge in an intellectual construct of my own for years and knew this was a dead end. It is not possible to experience commitment and faith toward an intellectual construct. It was no wonder that this construct was failing to satisfy my seeking. In between these two alternatives there was the Christian God about whom I had studied, and about whom my friends were speaking—God who is both removed from people and at the same time personal—and by virtue of the latter quality, in my mind, contradictory. How could God have personal attributes such as faithfulness? Would God then be anything more than a glorified man? Jesus as fully human and fully divine was even harder to understand or accept. I was too blinded by my own ego to see God, and too busy shutting God out to make sense of any of this.

With my daughter's decisions, I felt like a complete failure as a mother. This failure cast a shadow on my whole life. I feared for my child's safety. I tried to find out where she was, but was unable to do so, as our common contacts would not tell me. As an adult, she was entitled to her life but she was still a child in my mind—barely turned eighteen. I blamed everything on the leader of her group. I hated him with a burning intensity. In the meantime, she had left the group and was working part-time, although I was unaware of it.

I had not stopped sending emails to my daughter, hoping that she read them. Sometimes I would call the place where I heard she now worked, but it seemed clear she wanted me to leave her alone. I struggled to stay afloat. Burying myself in my work kept me going, but I was deeply unhappy. It seemed as though I was barely alive. I did what I knew best, turning to books to provide me with the skills and knowledge that would help me deal with these crises. I kept on believing that with the right book I would be fine! I frequented the Self-Help section of Borders, and Barnes & Noble.

The relief I would get from a book would be short-lived. I would try to occupy my mind with other thoughts, by immersing myself in other distractions such as television, or doing something physically strenuous like hiking. I would try to spend more time in the company of friends or coworkers, so that I could avoid thinking about my daughter. There was a period when I took down and put away all reminders of my daughter—books, photographs, and anything she had left with me. I tried to avoid talking to relatives. I was sure they would want to know where she was and what she was doing. But no matter how hard I tried, I could not get away from the reality of phone calls that went nowhere, emails that were never answered, and the heavy, opaque, all-consuming awareness of having failed as a mother, and losing someone forever—someone I loved more than anyone else in the world. Gone.

My boat was sinking, and I might never have surfaced had it not been for the fact that God was watching out for me.

5

Intervention

A<small>LMOST AS</small> if in preparation for my life crisis, I had met and married a man named Mike, whom I regard as one of God's greatest blessings in my life. With everything that I was going through, and the consequent emotional roller coaster I was riding, my new marriage should have fallen apart. Instead, it turned out to be a protected, love-filled space in my life that kept me from going under. Marrying again had never been in my plans. When Mike proposed, every logical bone in my body screamed no, telling me to run. Yet my deepest intuition told me this was a leap of faith I needed to take, and that Mike was a gift. I am so glad I went with this feeling. Mike has been my rock and my pillar of strength through the worst times of my life. During the crisis with my daughter, he provided me with reassurance, strength, and love. Above all, he was patient and understanding, giving me what I most needed—the time and space to figure things out. He frequently reminded me that I was not solely to blame for everything that had happened, and that I should not be so hard on myself. Through humor and love, he helped me retain my sanity and a modicum of faith in myself. However, he could not solve my problems. I needed a much greater power to fix me up and make me whole again. I finally understood this, and set off to look for God. I realized that Hinduism had brought me as far as was possible, and that there were some questions for which answers lay outside its offerings. For the first time in my life, I was really being open and listening. I was being awakened to God's grace, one step at a time.

On the radio, I heard about a book entitled *The Language of God*[1] written by Francis Collins, a scientist on the Human Genome Project. Collins wrote this book for people who struggle with a way to reconcile the findings of scientific research and the Christian concept of a personal Creator God. The author draws upon the works of C.S. Lewis where objections to faith are examined.[2] Collins' book, and the resources to which he points, address some of the issues surrounding belief in God that pose stumbling blocks for intellectuals, including: the problem of evil, suffering, miracles, and the matter of Christ being both human and God. It was in that moment that I started to shake off the lethargy of my long spiritual slumber. I began to see that the assumptions I had made about Jesus and about his teachings might have been very far from the truth. I started to read more about Jesus, and began to look for a church near where I lived. Still, the first church I chose to attend was not a Christian one but a congregation of the Unitarian Universalist Association. Once again, I was leaning toward a group that mapped into the intellectual, rather than faith-based, emphasis that had characterized my life for several years now. I still held many ideas about Christianity that were derived from my encounters with the missionar-

1. Collins, *The Language of God*.
2. Ibid., 21.

ies of my youth. While one side of me wanted to explore Christianity, the other side found this desire a hard pill to swallow.

I spent about six months with the Unitarians before I realized that I was getting nowhere. The people I met were warm and wonderful, but church felt more like a social club than a place to talk about and with God. There were some in this particular church who told me they had been born and raised Christian but had left because they detested the creeds and commitments of being a Christian. I got the feeling that several of the members had come from fundamentalist churches. There appeared to be a tone of political correctness that went with the need to be all things to all people and to cater to people of all religions. I felt we were just skimming the surface of faith-based questions. Our explorations never seemed to go anywhere. I left and continued seeking answers on my own. Once more, I explored faiths I had studied when I was younger, such as Buddhism. I even visited a Buddhist Sangha, and participated in the Buddhist practice of contemplation.

During this time, I still could not shut off the hubbub in my brain. My mind was pummeled by questions for which no answers were forthcoming. I knew there had to be an explanation for all that I was experiencing. I knew God was out there, and I wanted to find God. It was hard to find a quiet spot where I could take refuge even for a few minutes. No matter what I was doing, or how busy I kept myself, I could not turn off the guilt and the emptiness that I felt. Despite Mike's reminders to the contrary, I could not find anything of value in the person I had become. I could not forgive myself, and as a result, I had great difficulty forgiving people who had hurt or let me down in my life. I was dragging around a heavy load of baggage. Mike would sometimes joke, "Lose your baggage. Just give it to Delta!"

God then threw me a few more lifelines. Little by little, God was drawing me in and my life started to change. Everything I had read about Jesus in my childhood, studied in college, and heard from the Christian friends with whom I so vehemently argued, was starting to fall into place in my mind, in a series of progressive awakenings. These awakenings were like the appearance of missing pieces of a gigantic jigsaw puzzle. God in God's boundless grace was waking me up—despite everything I had done to remain in a faithless stupor—to comprehend God's love and message.

It started with a viewing of the movie *The Passion of the Christ*.[3] I knew this had been a controversial film, but my interest was focused on Jesus. I was shocked and appalled by the fact that Jesus did not just opt out, and find more congenial climes and locales to preach his ideas. My mind kept asking why. Who would want to undergo what he went through?

Next, I visited a Christian church close to where I lived: St. Hugh of Lincoln, an Episcopal church in Elgin, Illinois. The following week—as I was pondering the sermon I had heard—the pastor, Reverend Tom Atamian, mailed me a book entitled *Simply Christian*.[4] Pastor Tom followed that up each subsequent week with yet another great book by N.T. Wright, and several by John Stott, including the one I mentioned at the outset: *Why I Am a Christian*. Each of these books referred and drew me to other books. While

3. Gibson, *The Passion of the Christ*.
4. Wright, *Simply Christian*.

surfing the Web I came across the words to the Apostles' Creed.[5] When I came to the line that reads: "he descended into hell,"[6] a chill ran through me. Jesus did not just die and go to heaven. He went to hell first. I found myself thinking, "What Jesus went through in being crucified was real suffering undergone by Jesus as a man but his suffering was *huge* as it resulted from bearing the sin of all of mankind." When my daughter rejected me, the pain was unbearable. Yet that pain was trivial compared to what Jesus underwent by dying for me and for every sinner in the world! In that moment I finally understood that Jesus was no mere man, and that he was man and God. Looking back, this was a turning point in my journey to finding Jesus, and finding myself.

In the local library, I found a book on the topic of resurrection entitled *The Resurrection of Jesus: John Dominic Crossan and N.T. Wright in Dialogue*,[7] containing the perspectives of systematic theologians from different Christian denominations. I was particularly fascinated by the essay by the Reverend Dr. Ted Peters,[8] from the Pacific Lutheran Theological Seminary in Berkeley, California. I started to research the different denominations within Christianity, and felt drawn toward the Lutheran standpoint. My husband Mike had been raised Lutheran, but was not a practicing

5. Evangelical Lutheran Church in America, "The Apostles' Creed."

6. Ibid., line 3. Additionally, for an exploration of the meaning of this line in terms of the universal scope of salvation, see Pannenberg, *The Apostles' Creed in Light of Today's Questions*, 90–95.

7. Stewart, *The Resurrection of Jesus*.

8. Peters, "The Future of the Resurrection," 149–69.

Christian at the time. In any event, I decided to visit a congregation of the Evangelical Lutheran Church in America (ELCA) located nearby. It was Hosanna! Lutheran Church.

The final awakening that led to my baptism happened when I attended my first service at Hosanna!. I was sitting in the sanctuary a few minutes before the Saturday evening service was set to begin, when I became aware of a feeling of great peace coming upon me. The frenetic train of thoughts that had perpetually plagued my restless mind had been replaced by a sense of deep calmness. I felt as if Jesus was speaking softly to me saying, "Welcome home." The burden of anger, guilt, blame, and failure that I had carried for years was gone! It seemed as if a personal dialogue with God was the most natural thing in the world. I felt God's grace pouring over me. I felt accepted, loved and lifted. Above all, I felt forgiven. In those moments, I finally understood that even I had been spoken for when Jesus died on the cross. The meaning of redemption and grace finally broke through. A sense of utter gratitude, faith, and joyfulness filled me. In his sermon that day, Pastor John Nelson spoke about using one's gifts in the service of the Lord. I felt as if Jesus himself was speaking to me through Pastor John. I knew then that I needed, wanted, and had to be baptized. I arranged to meet the pastor. After a long conversation, where I felt right at home, a date was chosen. I was baptized on June 10, 2007 at Hosanna! Lutheran Church at the Sunday morning worship service. I knew I could have had a private ceremony, but I wanted to share my joy with the congregation. To my amazement and joy, my husband Mike stepped forward to be my sponsor.

My baptism was the highest moment in my entire life. Not too long thereafter, I began to discern the call to ordained ministry. I have developed a deep enriching relationship with God through prayer. I still feel the same exhilaration I felt on the day on which I came to know Christ. I feel it every day of my life. My life has been utterly transformed. Mike has returned to the church as an active member, and has been serving in numerous capacities, including that of worship leader.

Ever since my baptism, I have become more aware of the blessing of each day. Many miracles have come to pass. One such miracle is that my daughter and I have once again reunited and our family has been healed. I had always thought that after so much anger and bitterness, my relationship with my daughter was lost forever. God has watched over her, keeping her safe in this world of trouble and danger, and bringing her life around full circle. Her own life has been an awesome faith journey touched by God's grace. She is happily married and is now the mother of my grandson. My cup of happiness overflows. I know now that God has been preparing me, and has been faithful to me through all these trials and tribulations—despite my resistance to God's knocking on my door.

6

Transformation in Christ

THE IDEA of religious conversion is hard to grasp, and difficult to express in words. For many it is a source of discomfort, and even anger. Conversion is not something any human being can bring about, but an action that happens solely through God's work. It is something that must be personally experienced. What happened to me because of Christ was a total transformation, an experience of renewal that changed my whole life.

At the start of my journey in faith, I was a Hindu, and person who questioned the idea of religious conversion. My misgivings about conversion arose out of the conviction I held at the time that it is up to an individual to choose to believe in God, and the manner in which one expresses this belief in God. Hinduism, the religion of my childhood and upbringing, was undoubtedly instrumental in bringing me closer to God. It had led me to a point where I searched for God in many places, believing that the darkness that enveloped me would be rent by the rays of self-knowledge. But after a long and meandering journey through many shades of religious experience, I was far from satisfied on any level—intellectual, emotional or spiritual. It took the intervention of God in and through Jesus Christ to rescue me from the pit of hopelessness into which I had fallen.

I had thought that through my own powers of intellectual inquiry I would be able to reach and claim God. However, God cannot be accommodated within the meager dimensions of human understanding. With God's gracious initiative and involvement, however, we are brought into faith. We are able to place our trust in God. We are empowered to get glimpses of God's majesty and to appreciate what we mean to God. It is not we who find God but God who meets us where we are. The circumstances for this are different for each of us. For a scientist, it might be the inner workings of a cell where God's infinite creative glory comes to awaken and grow faith. For others, it is in the midst of an unbearable crisis that faith is born. God's grace comes to us through created means.

The story I described to you in the last chapter does not do justice to the many witnesses for Christ who became these created means of grace: a colleague who, knowing I was in a personal crisis, took the bold step of suggesting passages from the Bible that I might read, at the risk of being insulted or ignored; friends who supported me through listening and prayer; pastors who gave me food for thought, and whose hospitality was never laced with ulterior motives; personal stories shared with me by complete strangers whom I met on business trips on airplanes, which led me to ponder who I really was, and where I was really going; the warmth I received from members of congregations I visited; and the love of my husband Mike, whose honesty and humor kept me going even when things appeared very bleak.

Regardless of how or where God meets us, one thing that we can be certain of is that God loves and cares for creation so deeply that God comes and claims us, and brings us home, although we have wandered very far and have become lost. For me, as for others, God's presence in the midst of my personal suffering made it possible to endure what seemed intolerably painful, and led to healing and reconciliation. What does my baptism in Christ mean to me? Why am I a Christian? Here are some thoughts I wrote down in the week leading up to my baptism.

No other figure, historical or mythological, demands our belief and obedience in as powerful a way as Jesus. This is because his story is a story of love and compassion. No other figure is as commanding, as compelling or as meaningful as he is, because he lived what he preached. Some religions promise that through knowledge we will be freed from pain and pleasure. Others urge us to seek the destruction of our selfhood. But the experiential joy and glory of the life Christ offers us, here and hereafter, are infinitely more appealing to me than a dry, intellectual salvation.

Some religions allow for "many ways" to reach God. This sentiment sounds enticing, but it makes God subject to human endeavor. While other religions can be sources of revelation, Jesus Christ alone is the definitive and salvific revelation of God. By becoming human and being with us, God enables us to reach God. Christ's faithfulness unto death on the cross and his triumph over death and sin through his resurrection make it clear to us that we cannot absorb the power and holiness of God without total immersion in God's Word. To be Christian is to accept the gift of God in Christ, and express our discipleship in unswerving loyalty and commitment to God. We cannot comprehend the meaning of his message if we are not fully ready to follow God's commandments. We cannot give a half-hearted nod, nor refuse to acknowledge Jesus' life as our creed, and still expect to reach God.

God created us to live in community with one another, and with all of creation. When we sing God's praise in worship or read God's word together, we get a sense of God's greatness. We share this vision with each other as a congregation joined together in God's love and teaching. This shared sense of awe is similar to the feeling we experience on a mountain or on the seashore. We revel in the beauty of creation in the faces of our children, in the birds, and in the trees. Unlike religions that emphasize ritual purity and ceremonial precision, Christian worship focuses on Christ and our personal bond with Him, as one people of God. We take this unique bond we feel as followers of Jesus as we go about our everyday lives.

God forgives us over and over, when we in our brokenness go astray yet again. Jesus releases us from the burden of guilt when we acknowledge that we have sinned. This admission is the first step we take towards changing our lives for the better, by making the right choices. Shedding this burden allows us to see our fellow human beings and ourselves in a new light, without prejudices and preconceptions. We are called to forgive others, just as God forgives us. We exchange our egos for the freedom of following Christ's commandments. Our fates are not sealed by our birth into a particular caste or class. Nor are we lulled into a false sense of perfection we have not attained.

Jesus' real suffering and his transcendence over death and evil illustrate to us that we too can triumph over things and events that try to trap us into taking the path of least resistance. Jesus could have opted out anytime during his trial before Pontius Pilate, but he did not. By suffering on the cross, he set us up to receive his grace. This miracle alone denies me any excuse to waver in my faith. God's gift to me, undeserving as I am, inspires me to turn my life around through real changes, and take responsibility for who I am. No other religion I know gives me this guarantee of redemption.

As a Christian, I feel the loving acceptance of my congregation, just as I accept every one of them as children of God. There is no reason why I am inferior to someone else. I am beautiful as I am, whether I am black, brown or white, tall, short, outgoing or shy. My past does not define me. Where I come from or what I do for a living are of no import. Living in Christ is all that matters. Despite our very real shortcomings, we are all lovable because God loves each and every one of us.

To realize that we cannot do without God is an awesome, freeing realization. Some religions fight shy of acknowledging the need for a personal God. Others avoid the use of the word God because it may be politically incorrect. Yet others suspend belief. Christians unequivocally declare their dependence on God, and in so doing realize the utter happiness and freedom that comes from laying their burdens at God's feet. When we are not afraid to ask for help, we are able to find the strength we never knew we had.

When we embrace God's gift of grace in and through Jesus, we cannot help feeling that we want to release our ego into the vastness of God's love. We wish we could be more like Christ, loving our neighbors, coworkers, and family members alike. We want to give back to the community that supports us, and try in our own small way to express the gratitude we feel for our being justified by God's grace. We desperately seek to engage our particular gifts in work that glorifies God's name. We rejoice in the gifts of others. We experience the joy of servanthood in Christ.

God does not desert us even in our darkest moments. Because of this, we can find reasons for which to be thankful, and take comfort in the knowledge that God's boundless grace surrounds us always. We may not understand everything or see the whole picture, but we can rest assured that the time of adversity will pass. God has already proved God's loyalty and love for us through the cross.

We know we have one chance—this life—and we need to make the most of it. Through the work of the Holy Spirit, each one of us now has the power to change the course of our lives. We cannot rely on transmigration or operate on a cosmic sense of time. We must make the right choices now, finding happiness and peace in God's plan for us. We are called to live out God's direction to us to love one another and serve one another, as disciples of Jesus. We have no justification for delaying our good acts. Made righteous by God's gift, we are empowered to come together to ensure justice for all.

7

Who is God?

M Y CONVERSION experience did not lead me to dis-cover a new God, switch allegiances to a different God, or to know God for the first time. In fact, I did not find God. God had been caring for me all along and now revealed Godself to me. I learned that it mattered greatly whom I identified as God. I came to see why it ultimately proved so hard for me to be a believer as a Hindu. People from different religions can often agree that God speaks to each of us in different ways, but they seem to have difficulty agreeing that there is only one God. Why is this so?

As a Hindu, I had often wondered: Why were Christians so adamant that their God was the one true God? Why couldn't we just agree to disagree? They could keep their God, and I could keep mine! What was wrong with saying that I conceive of God a certain way that is uniquely mine, and that you conceive of God in a different way that is uniquely yours? Since God cannot be fully contained by either of our human conceptions, why not just allow for the validity of both of these conceptions? But even then, I knew that there was only one God, which is why my parents and I were quite comfortable worshiping in a church or in a temple. Because of this, I am optimistic that members of my extended family who are still Hindu will understand where I stand, and continue to further ponder the basis of the beliefs that let them feel a connection to God through Christ. My desire is for them to know Christ more deeply than they might so far have done. There is a richness and depth of faith that awaits them.

When I look back on my journey in faith, I see that I started from the fundamental Hindu belief that there are many ways to reach God—as many ways as there are people. I had a problem with the statement that Jesus alone was the way to God, because I interpreted Jesus as one way of getting to God among many others. Buddha was another. Mohammed was yet another. Along with this was the Hindu assumption that there can be many conceptions of God. Since Hinduism is a very ancient religion with multiple cultural streams blending into it, each of these cultures brought to it a different understanding of God. Perhaps because of the underlying assumption that it is perfectly acceptable to have more than one conception of God, a variety of belief systems developed side by side within this religion along with the many forms in which God is conceived.

There is only one God, and God was God all along. Awakened by Christ, I see now that God is not an abstract entity but is Triune—in three distinct relationships with the world: God is the Father, God is the Son (the Word made incarnate in Jesus Christ), and God is the Holy Spirit which moves among and within us and every created being.[1] God

1. World Council of Churches. *Confessing the One Faith.* This book offers a detailed, ecumenical explication of a core, Christian credal statement—the Nicene-Constantinopolitan Creed, clarifying what it meant by "Triune," and highlighting the ways in which the

speaks to us in many ways—through a variety of created means, by the work of the Holy Spirit. These are the people and circumstances in which we are placed, and for each of us this is unique and tailor-made. God prepares each one of us differently, according to the gifts with which God has blessed us. In Lesslie Newbigin's words: "God's self-revelation in Jesus is not simply an event which recedes farther and farther into the past; through the work of the Spirit we are led into an ever fuller understanding of it as the Spirit takes of the things of Jesus and shows them to us through the experiences of our place and time."[2]

When I was a Hindu, I mistook Jesus to be one way among others. I now clearly understand why Jesus cannot be relegated to a plane that is on par with such created means as Buddha or Mohammed. Being fully human and fully divine, Jesus is the Creator—not the created. Buddha, Mohammed, or any of the symbols of Hinduism, all of which are created means, can lead us to God, if and only if they lead us to Jesus. For it is only in the experience of God's grace in this intimately personal way— through the life, crucifixion, death, and resurrection of Jesus—that we encounter God.

If we examine the many diverse schools of thought inside Hinduism, we can see a continuing unrest in its core, with succeeding generations of thinkers attempting to come up with a more satisfactory conception of God. In these attempts to define God, there is a very real sense that something is missing. Interestingly, instead of each new attempt replacing what went before, God continued to be

Trinitarian affirmation of Christians has been misunderstood.

2. Newbigin, *The Gospel in a Pluralist Society*, 164.

seen in different ways, side by side: in nature as a whole in a pantheistic way, in particular animals, in imaginary creatures based on mythology, and in non-personal, abstract ways. Advaita Vedanta is the most developed and internally consistent of these attempts because this school recognizes that truth does not come in many flavors, and that the many gods and goddesses are not ultimately real. However, in this process, one loses touch with the personal nature of God. The school turns to the individual's search for self-knowledge as the way to understand the nature of reality. Through the path of knowledge, the individual was thought to be able to somehow escape the bounds of his or her mind, and grasp the one, non-dual nature of ultimate reality. However, first, it is difficult to explain how such a leap can occur, and second, God gets lost in the idea of reality being a sea of consciousness. Thus does God become an abstraction, one that remains forever out of reach.

In his attempt to systematize Hinduism and explain Advaita, Shankara was motivated by the desire to stamp out social injustices such as untouchability that resulted from the Hindu caste system. He tried to show that everyone is equal, in that everyone is essentially of the nature of consciousness, and that any differences between individuals—including ideas generated by wealth and privileged birth—are an illusion. Despite his efforts, the parallel streams of Hindu thinking about our essential nature persisted, and the injustices he fought could not be eradicated. It seems to me that Shankara's efforts to get rid of social injustices failed because, ultimately, he could not point to a compelling reason for a given individual to render justice unto others. Such a compelling reason can only come from the authority and commitment that comes from receiving Jesus as a friend and savior, and from the understanding that all of creation is precious to God, and each individual is unique and real.

After Shankara, attempts to come up with a more satisfactory way to explain God—particularly one that has a bearing on everyday life—appear to have all but died out within Hinduism. A relativism about God appears to have set in, and it is almost as if how God is conceived does not matter.

As I said earlier, the idea that we can each have our own conception of God is very attractive. I held on to it for the longest time. However, even within a single religion such as Hinduism, it is problematic for several reasons. Between two different religions, it gets even more complex. From a purely logical standpoint, we might all see that there cannot be more than one Supreme Being. A Hindu might argue that it is not a matter of "many flavors of truth" but that no two people can see the whole truth, but only aspects of it. We might start out acknowledging this, but things get complicated. In our human brokenness, we cannot help but impose boundaries on the God we create in our minds. Soon the line between my particular idea of God and the understanding that God is much more than my understanding begins to blur. We put God in a box, and now each side is invested in proving that their God is the real McCoy.

Within Hinduism, there were always worshippers of the god Shiva pitted against the worshippers of the god Vishnu, or the worshippers of the goddess Devi. It did not help that the gods competed with each other even within the stories of Hindu mythology. Sooner or later, a devotee of one god would move to the position that, in worshipping a lesser god, the other was now less worthy of respect than otherwise. Some Hindus simply chose not to take sides, and just prayed to as many of these gods as they could, just to maximize the chances of prayers being heard. This was the world in which I grew up, with my parents expressing their amusement at the silliness of such arguments. They definitely leaned toward the view that the polytheism embedded in Hindu mythology was to be taken with a grain of salt.

I had a choice in how I could understand the gods and goddesses of Hinduism. I could treat all the gods and goddesses as ultimately real, but this lead to the problems associated with polytheism. The very meaning of the word God or Supreme Being entails a single entity not many, forcing me to subscribe to one or the other as the supreme God. So which one should I pick? Alternatively, I could use the explanation provided by my parents, namely, that the gods and goddesses were just forms we use to approach God, and these forms were not ultimately real. Now I can see how over time my individualistic conception of God as pure existence—an abstraction—rather than one that is essentially relational, that is includes personhood, had come to be.

I earlier narrated how I pulled away from pluralism, being attracted to the definition of God as pure existence-consciousness-bliss. But this school of thought was all up in the head, with no heart. The idea of a personal God began to recede further and further and I was left with an intellectual construct. Praying to an intellectual construct is rather difficult. From there it was an easy slide to believing

I was fine without prayer, since there was nothing or no one listening anyway. I was intelligent, and capable of figuring things out on my own. I did not have to admit to a total and unavoidable dependence on a higher power. There was no limit to my understanding, and I made God an artifact that belonged inside the vast space of my intellectual potential.

However, we get our value and our direction from the God whom we worship. Hence, our understanding of God is entirely tied to who we are as people. When I placed God in the category of intellectual constructs that are helpful for a while and can later be discarded, my understanding of God was as strong as the abstraction in my mind. Between my urge to believe that I was in control, and my deeply embedded confusion about who God really is, I replaced God with the self-gratifying idol of education for that is where I felt secure. But when the chips are down, our idols do not supply us with strength, courage, or compassion. They offer nothing, and their assurance is revealed to be empty. I have tried to describe this in my story.

When our conception of God is defined solely by our minds, it no longer has any real impact on our daily lives. Such a concept of God did not inspire me to be accepting of others, or ultimately accepting of myself. Driven by the ideal of gaining perfect knowledge, I was continually dissatisfied with myself, and the world in which I lived. I analyzed, rather than experienced, God. I had no need for scripture unless the scripture fit in with my understanding of God. So busy was I searching for peace of mind in the wrong places that I drifted further and further away from the true source of peace and joy. Many people today find themselves in a similar predicament.

There was also another reason why I could not relate to God in any significant way in Hinduism. The many forms of God in Hinduism ultimately failed to hold my faith, because God remained unrelated to my life here on earth, and I could not find a way to bridge the gap. Hinduism cannot conceive of God as someone who would choose to be a part of this imperfect world, out of love for creation. Even when God takes an incarnation, God in Hinduism remains strictly God and does not suffer the shortcomings of our world. The idea of a God who is entirely removed from the world and its suffering makes it hard to understand our own suffering. In this case, we are forced to choose between a God who does not care about our suffering, and one who even takes delight in making us suffer. Neither alternative is satisfactory. Neither is compelling.

When I was Hindu, I felt that if there was a God out there, and it was up to me to make some effort to remain on its good side. I felt more like a child who is forced to be nice to her classmates out of fear for the consequences, than a member of a mutually caring and compassionate community. I did not feel any sense of being loved by God for who I was as an individual. God was a powerful force who could be my ally, but it was up to me to take the initiative. To resolve the problem of evil, I described earlier how Hinduism uses the theory of *karma*. Even God does not intervene in the realm of *karma*. The individual is forever trapped in the cycle of birth and rebirth due to the effects of *karma*, and getting out of this cycle is well nigh impossible. And if God cannot alter *karma*, then is God really God? Interestingly, Alouben, a Christian missionary who went to China during the Tang

dynasty, preached about Christ to the Buddhists he encountered as one who could redeem the sinner from *karma*.[3]

Thus, who our God is matters greatly. It defines who
we are, who we are in relationship to this God, and who
we are to other created beings. God cannot be God unless
God demands our obedience through love, acceptance, and
compassion. God cannot be God unless we have a way to
look to God for forgiveness when we make mistakes—and
make mistakes we unavoidably will, in our brokenness.
God cannot be God unless we can find redemption in God's
eternal mercy and grace. For all this to be possible, God
needs to be personal, essentially relational, and want to
have a relationship with us.

It is on account of the grace of the one, Triune, essentially relational God who is faithful to us to eternity that
we are justified, and feel called as justified beings, to be just
to each other. I must love you, not because God sets an example by loving me, but because you are God's beloved as
much as I am, and because we have been created to live in
community, loving one another.

Without Christ, we have no access to God because
God cannot be comprehended by our finite intellects. Being
fully human and fully divine, Christ completes the circle
and fills the gap between the incomprehensible mystery of
God and us in a way no shade of individual religious experience without Christ ever could. Because Jesus is fully
human and fully divine, he bridges the yawning chasm that
divides us—in our brokenness—from God. On the flip side,
I am convinced that wherever there is a mystic who has en-

3. Palmer, *The Jesus Sutras*, 137–38.

countered God, in whatever religion he or she might be, there Jesus Christ must be as well.

It is through God's initiative, not ours, that our spiritual life has its beginning. Because of this, the scriptures of different religions can speak to us about God and draw us closer to this understanding, and eventually, to a personal encounter with Jesus. Thus we can find Jesus in the scriptures of other religions, and people who have not yet tasted the grace of Christ, can find their way to him, through means of grace that exist within their reach. For God watches over all, and no one is excluded from God's grace. My experience of being born and raised in Hinduism, and then being brought into the grace of God through Jesus is my testimony to what I have expressed above.

8

Who Am I?

THANKS TO Christ's intervention in my life, I have to come to understand that each one of us is created to live this one life in community with the rest of creation, and not as an isolated, individual soul floating through countless lives on its lonely journey.

When I was a Hindu, I remember that my family and I were amused by stories of individuals converting to Christianity. My brother once remarked: "Converts are more Christian than Christians themselves." It was difficult to understand why someone who was formerly Hindu and now Christian was so heavily invested in reading the Bible, attending church, participating in study groups, and constantly talking about community as the "body of Christ." As Hindus, we simply did not understand the idea of fellowship and community. Not having experienced Jesus, we could not understand the convert's experience. I believe that our lukewarm responses toward God and our judgmental responses to each other were another consequence of the idea that there can be many ways to reach God.

Hinduism was a religion of convenience for me. I was not committed to following anything but the most generic of values. I could not understand the singular, unwavering faith and commitment of believers in Christ. Nor could I understand their passion for evangelism. The entry of Jesus into my life has helped me understand that while God speaks to us in different ways, pouring God's grace on us through a variety of created means, it is in and through Jesus that we are able to have a personal, life-giving relationship with God, a relationship that radically transforms our lives.

It was not until I myself became a Christian that I understood that, for a Christian, not talking about Christ is akin to knowing about a treasure and not being willing to share the knowledge. Jesus had been knocking on my door for a long time, but I had paid him no heed, believing that knowledge was the key to happiness. I took the path that led to disillusionment, and had to hit rock bottom before I realized that my happiness lay in surrendering myself to Christ. As an intellectual, I could not be happy, because no matter how much knowledge I gathered, it was never enough. I continued to fall short of my own expectations. Unable to love and accept myself, I could not fully love and accept anyone else. Once Christ found me, and through grace accepted me for what I was—with all my shortcomings and imperfections—I realized I had found the key to happiness, and I wanted to tell the whole world about it. Jesus' great commission is for us to do just this, to announce the good news of the reign of God to the ends of the earth. In his life, Jesus exemplifies this message by his radical call to follow him, and in so doing open up every door that we had previously kept closed, barred, and locked.

Encountering Jesus has radically altered my understanding of who I am. It has changed how I regard the life I have been given and what I expect after this life is done.

Lutheran theologian Carl E. Braaten says: "Jesus never talked about gradual measures, minor improvements, piecemeal changes, or just a little bit of progress. He had an all-or-nothing way of speaking. He was not for reform, but repentance, not for accommodation but conversion."[1]

Conversion is an expression of a life transformation encountered as the converted person grapples with the very meaning of existence. In many ways, it is a life-long process. Even after God breaks down the walls we erect around ourselves, we in our brokenness try to build new ones. Once we have experienced God in Christ, we continue to have—through further experiences—an ongoing and deeper awakening about who we are, who God is, and how we stand in relationship with God. God accepts us and repeatedly forgives us, even as we begin to have an appreciation of God's faithfulness to us. I had a dire need to experience God's grace. I had a need to believe in God's promise to bring us safely to salvation. In and through Christ Jesus alone did I find the fulfillment of my seeking. I hope my testimony helps you understand what the words of John 14:6 mean to me: "Jesus said to him, 'I am the way, and the truth, and the life. No one comes to the Father except through me.'"[2]

Because of Christ, I have the personal experience of a God who emptied Godself for me. Jesus' faithfulness on the cross speaks for God's faithfulness to me, despite the many times I have turned away from God. In my idolatry, I was sucked into a depleting and hopeless void and cut myself off from God, the source of all life and wholeness. God, in and through Jesus, took the initiative to retrieve me, and

1. Braaten, *That All May Believe*, 129.
2. John 14:6 (New Revised Standard Version).

gave me yet another chance to fulfill the purpose for which I was created.

Most of us are ready to make sacrifices for the sake of those who are near and dear to us. But Jesus calls for us to widen our understanding of family, and to be ready to give up our cherished rights for the sake of the good of the larger community. It is that kind of commitment that makes the difference between a world in which justice is available for all and one in which some will forever remain outside the circle. Touched by God's grace in and through Jesus, we are called to make a similar, unequivocal commitment to walk his ways and be like him.

Community as Christians experience it is strikingly different from its counterpart in Hinduism. Although traditionally Hindus revere community, it is a very individualistic religion. Prayer, for example, is a very private matter and there is nothing quite like the corporate intercessory prayer that forms a part of the core worship in church as part of Christian communities coming together to worship God. The idea of *karma* is based on the understanding that it is up to each person to seek their own liberation from the cycle of birth and death. For Christians, there is an imperative to be a community together, to build each other up, and to be loving and kind toward each other, and not judgmental. Jesus—through his actions—demands this of us. Our response of obedience to Jesus is a response to his love toward us, proven repeatedly.

What does it mean to live in Jesus? It means that we can see light even in the darkest of situations. We can see good in people even when their actions seem misguided. In hindsight, I feel thankful even to the homeless man who mistakenly thought he was the second coming of Jesus. He had been the object of my anger for many years, for his role in my daughter's rejection of formal education. But I can see that while he might have been deluded, he had a good side, and my daughter learned a lot about Jesus through this man. Those seeds would eventually take root and bring God's message to her, years after she had left the company of the man.

Living in Jesus means that I do not have to give up who I am to gain salvation. I do not have to discard the body and mind I have been given and return to a pure state of consciousness that is devoid of everything that defines me as a person, before I can enjoy communion with God. With Jesus, I do not need to postulate numerous lives over the course of which I can make my way to salvation. Jesus loves me as I am in my brokenness, and welcomes me home always. Neither an abstract, intellectual idea of salvation nor a picture of disembodied souls in a distant paradise can comfort me as Jesus can. In Jesus alone lies my salvation.

By loving and serving you, I serve him who gave his life for both of us. Because of Jesus, I can experience the kingdom of God right here right now. In the death and resurrection of Jesus, the reign of God has begun. I do not have to wait for a distant time and place. I do not have to escape this world or this body to taste the peace of God. I can celebrate the earth and the life I have been given, until the day when we will be forever united with God.

In his writing "A Brief Instruction on What to Look for and Expect in the Gospels," Martin Luther explains: "The chief article and foundation of the gospel is that before you take Christ as an example, you accept and recognize him as a gift, as a present that God has given you and that is your own . . . . As widely as a gift differs from an example, so widely does faith differ from works, for faith possesses nothing of its own, only the deeds and life of Christ. Works have something of your own in them, yet they should not belong to you but to your neighbor."[3] God's gift in Christ—which expresses God's overwhelming love for us—so transforms us that we are now able to follow Christ's example, and be to our neighbor what Christ is to us. And it is faith alone, not our actions, that redeems us from sin and death.

What can be stronger or more compelling than the love that God in Jesus bears for me, a love so deep that he would undergo suffering, and death by crucifixion so that chaos would be replaced with the kingdom of God? Because of what Jesus underwent for me and for all of creation to be renewed, I know that he is present with anyone who suffers. Because of that, we are never alone, even in the darkest, more despairing times of our lives. It is the constant presence of Christ in our lives that lets us know we can count on him, and that he, unlike other fallible idols, will never let us down. It is through our identity as God's children, an identity we come to realize in and through Christ, that we are able to live life to its fullest, in harmony with one another and all of creation. God's grace is sufficient to overcome our human failings.

We cannot foresee God's plan for us, but that God has a plan is manifestly clear to me. Christ confers life, vitality, healing, and wholeness. Christ bears our burdens, and holds us in his arms when we are too weak to walk on our own. He invests us with the strength to overcome our tribulations, and to persevere in the calling that he gives us. Christ is the lifeline that guides us in the fog, and leads us to emerge again, from out of the fog, into the sun. Believing is transformation that is forever. All we have to do is hold on to Jesus.

3. Luther, "A Brief Instruction on What to Look for and Expect in the Gospels," 95.

9

The Journey Continues

I HOPE you have found the story of how and why I became Christian helpful in your own discernment. I pray that you experience the richness and joy that can only come through God's grace, and that you feel God's presence in your life. Since I started writing this book, I have felt a call to ordained ministry, and am now in the third year of my MDiv program. As our respective journeys continue, I thank God for bringing us together in the writing and the reading of this book.

Peace and Joy in Christ,
Jo Nageswaran Kinnard

Bibliography

Braaten, Carl E. *That All May Believe: A Theology of the Gospel and the Mission of the Church*. Grand Rapids: Eerdmans, 2008.

Collins, Francis S. *The Language of God: A Scientist Presents Evidence for Belief*. New York: Free Press, 2006.

Evangelical Lutheran Church in America. "The Apostles' Creed." No Pages. Online: http://www.elca.org/What-We-Believe/Statements-of-Belief/The-Apostles-Creed.aspx.

Gibson, Mel, director. *The Passion of the Christ*. DVD. Beverly Hills: 20th Century Fox Home Entertainment, 2004.

Luther, Martin. "A Brief Instruction on What to Look for and Expect in the Gospels." In *Martin Luther's Basic Theological Writings*, 2nd ed., edited by Timothy F. Lull and William R. Russell, 93–97. Minneapolis: Fortress, 2005.

Newbigin, Lesslie. *The Gospel in a Pluralist Society*. Grand Rapids: Eerdmans, 1989.

Palmer, Martin. *The Jesus Sutras: Rediscovering the Lost Scrolls of Taoist Christianity*. New York: Ballantine, 2001.

Pannenberg, Wolfhart. *The Apostles' Creed in Light of Today's Questions*. 1972. Reprint, Eugene: Wipf and Stock, 2000.

Peters, Ted. "The Future of the Resurrection." In *The Resurrection of Jesus: John Dominic Crossan and N.T. Wright in Dialogue*, edited by Robert B. Stewart, 149–69. Minneapolis: Fortress, 2006.

Russell, Bertrand. *Why I Am Not a Christian: And Other Essays on Religion And Related Subjects*. 7th cloth ed. New York: Simon and Shuster, 1963.

Stewart, Robert B. ed. *The Resurrection of Jesus: John Dominic Crossan and N.T. Wright in Dialogue*. Minneapolis: Augsburg Fortress, 2006.

Stott, John. *Why I Am a Christian*. Downer's Grove, IL: InterVarsity, 2003.

Tapasyananda, Swami, translator. *Srimad Bhagavad Gita: The Scripture of Mankind.* 1984. Reprint, Madras: Sri Ramakrishna Math, 1988.

World Council of Churches. *Confessing the One Faith: An Ecumenical Explication of the Apostolic Faith as It is Confessed in the Nicene-Constantinopolitan Creed (381).* 1991. Reprint, Geneva: WCC Publications, 1999.

Wright, N. T. *Simply Christian: Why Christianity Makes Sense.* New York: HarperCollins, 2006.